Dinosaur Detective
Search for the facts...

Archaeopteryx
and Other
Flying Reptiles

Tracey Kelly

raintree
a Capstone company — publishers for children

Raintree is an imprint of Capstone Global Library Limited, a company incorporated in England and Wales having its registered office at 264 Banbury Road, Oxford, OX2 7DY – Registered company number: 6695582

www.raintree.co.uk
myorders@raintree.co.uk

Text: Tracey Kelly
Designer: John Woolford
Design Manager: Keith Davis
Editorial Director: Lindsey Lowe
Children's Publisher: Anne O'Daly
Picture Manager: Sophie Mortimer
Production by Katie LaVigne
Printed and bound in India

ISBN 978 1 4747 7833 6 (hardback)
ISBN 978 1 4747 7839 8 (paperback)

British Library Cataloguing in Publication Data
A full catalogue record for this book is available from the British Library.

Acknowledgements
We would like to thank the following for permission to reproduce photographs:
Shutterstock: Mikhail SH 4.

Every effort has been made to contact copyright holders of material reproduced in this book. Any omissions will be rectified in subsequent printings if notice is given to the publisher.

Contents

How do we know about dinosaurs?

Scientists are like detectives.
They look at fossils.
Fossils tell us where dinosaurs
and other ancient animals lived.
They tell us how big they were.

This is an *Archaeopteryx* fossil. The first fossil was a feather. It was found in some rocks in Germany. Only 12 *Archaeopteryx* fossils have been found.

How to use this book

This tells you
what the
animal ate.

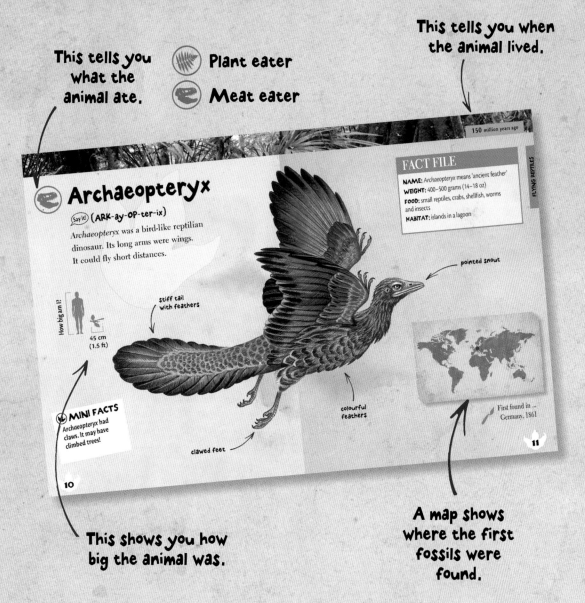

Plant eater

Meat eater

This tells you when
the animal lived.

150 million years ago

FLYING REPTILES

Archaeopteryx

Say it! (ARK-ay-OP-ter-ix)

Archaeopteryx was a bird-like reptilian
dinosaur. Its long arms were wings.
It could fly short distances.

FACT FILE

NAME: Archaeopteryx means 'ancient feather'
WEIGHT: 400–500 grams (14–18 oz)
FOOD: small reptiles, crabs, shellfish, worms
and insects
HABITAT: islands in a lagoon

pointed snout

How big am I?

45 cm
(1.5 ft)

stiff tail
with feathers

colourful
feathers

First found in ...
Germany, 1861

MINI FACTS
Archaeopteryx had
claws. It may have
climbed trees!

clawed feet

10

11

This shows you how
big the animal was.

A map shows
where the first
fossils were
found.

Read on to become a dinosaur detective!

Flying reptiles

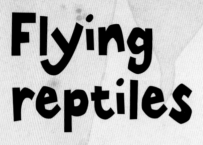

Pterosaurs (TEH-row-sores)
were flying reptiles. They lived
220 million years ago.
Pterosaurs were not dinosaurs.
But they lived at the same time.

Anurognathus

Say it! (ann-YOOR-rog-NAY-thus)

Anurognathus was a pterosaur. It had a small tail and body. It had leathery wings. It could change direction quickly.

sharp teeth for grabbing prey

MINI FACTS

Scientists have only found one *Anurognathus* skeleton.

FACT FILE

NAME: *Anurognathus* means 'tailless jaw'
LENGTH: up to 9 cm (3.5 in.)
WEIGHT: 40 g (1½ oz.)
FOOD: insects
HABITAT: forests near shallow lagoons

How big am I?

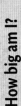
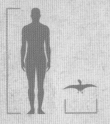

**50 cm (20 in.)
wingspan**

short fingers

light wings

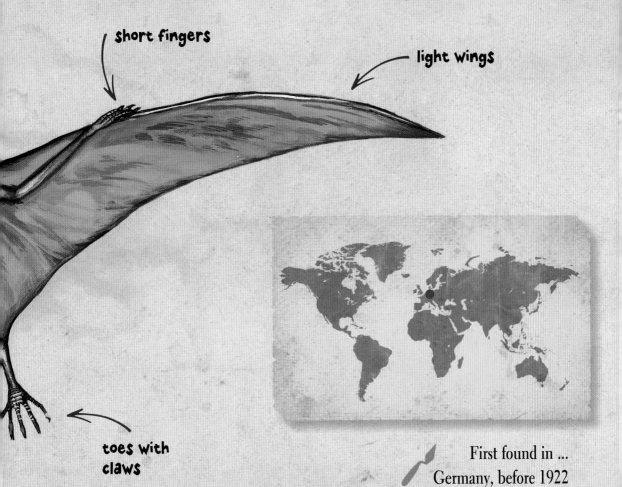

toes with
claws

First found in ...
Germany, before 1922

9

Archaeopteryx

Say it! (ARK-ay-OP-ter-ix)

Archaeopteryx was a bird-like dinosaur. Its long arms were wings. It could fly short distances.

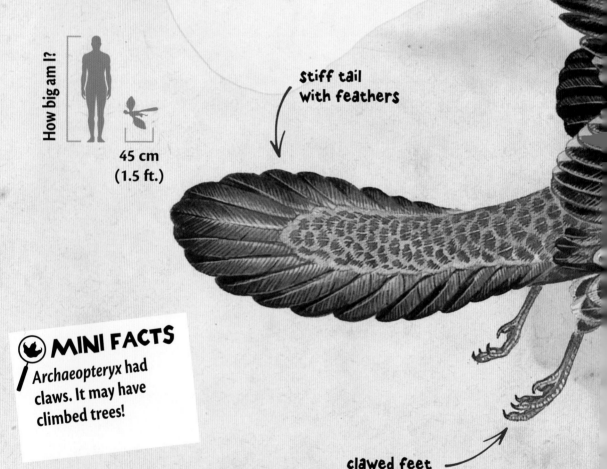

How big am I?

45 cm
(1.5 ft.)

Stiff tail with feathers

MINI FACTS

Archaeopteryx had claws. It may have climbed trees!

clawed feet

10

FACT FILE

NAME: *Archaeopteryx* means 'ancient feather'

WEIGHT: 400–500 g (14–18 oz.)

FOOD: small reptiles, crabs, shellfish, worms and insects

HABITAT: islands in a lagoon

pointed snout

colourful feathers

First found in ...
Germany, 1861

11

Dimorphodon

Say it! (dye-MORF-oh-DON)

Dimorphodon was a flying pterosaur. It had a huge head. Its front teeth were big. They stuck out of its beak.

claws used for grasping

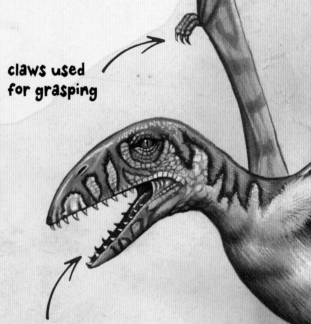

How big am I?

1.4 m (4.5 ft.) wingspan

long front teeth and tiny back teeth

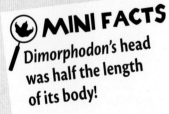

MINI FACTS

Dimorphodon's head was half the length of its body!

FACT FILE

NAME: *Dimorphodon* means 'two-form tooth'

LENGTH: up to 1 m (3 ft.)

FOOD: insects and small lizards

HABITAT: near coasts

long wings
made of skin

First found in ...
England, 1828

Eudimorphodon

Say it! (you-dye-MORF-oh-DON)

Eudimorphodon had a long beak.
It swooped low over the water.
Its sharp teeth snapped up fish.

MINI FACTS

Eudimorphodon
had about 55 teeth
in each jaw.

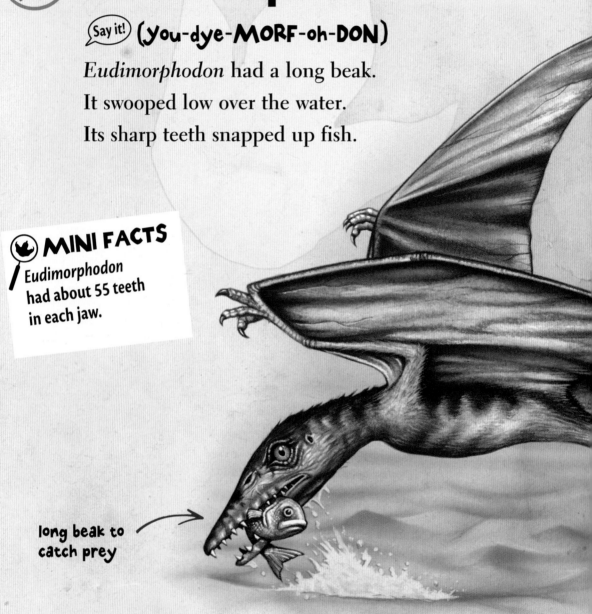

long beak to
catch prey

FLYING REPTILES

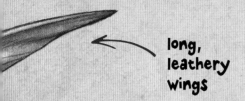

long, leathery wings

FACT FILE

NAME: *Eudimorphodon* means 'true two-form tooth'

WEIGHT: up to 9 kg (20 lbs.)

FOOD: fish, insects and small animals

HABITAT: shorelines

long tail

diamond-shaped tail flap

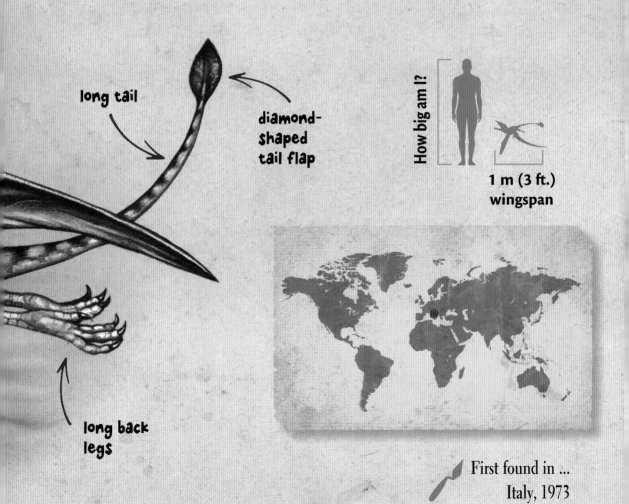

How big am I?

1 m (3 ft.) wingspan

long back legs

First found in ...
Italy, 1973

15

Kuehneosuchus

 Say it! (KOON-ee-oh-SOO-chus)

Kuehneosuchus was a small lizard. It had long wing flaps. It could glide from trees.

How big am I?

length 71 cm
(28 in.)

🐾 MINI FACTS

Kuehneosuchus had strong jaws. It snapped up insects.

strong jaws

long back legs
for running

FACT FILE

NAME: *Kuehneosuchus* means 'Keuhne's crocodile'

WINGSPAN: up to 40 cm (16 in.)

FOOD: insects

HABITAT: forests

First found in ...
England, 1962

wing flaps

Pterodactylus

 (TARE-oh-DAK-till-us)

Pterodactylus was a small pterosaur.
Its mouth was full of sharp teeth.
It hunted insects and fish.

✹ MINI FACTS

Pterodactylus could walk on the ground. It probably walked on all fours.

mouth had 90 teeth

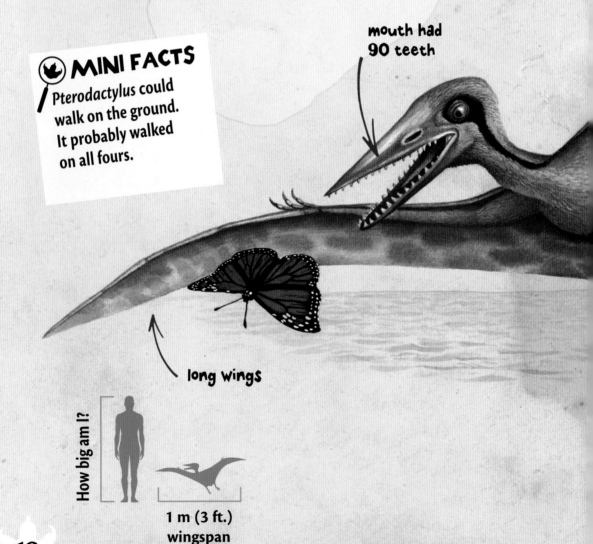

long wings

How big am I?

1 m (3 ft.) wingspan

long wing fingers

wing tip helped
to steer

FACT FILE

NAME: *Pterodactylus* means
'winged finger'

WEIGHT: about 4.5 kg (10 lbs.)

FOOD: insects, fish, shellfish and small lizards

HABITAT: shores and rivers

back legs
had claws

First found in ...
Germany, 1767–1784

Rhamphorhynchus

Say it! (RAM-for-RIN-kus)

Rhamphorhynchus had narrow wings.
It had a very long tail.
This made it a strong flyer.

How big am I?

1.8 m (6 ft.)
wingspan

spiky teeth

wing fingers

🔍 MINI FACTS

Rhamphorhynchus
nested in big groups.

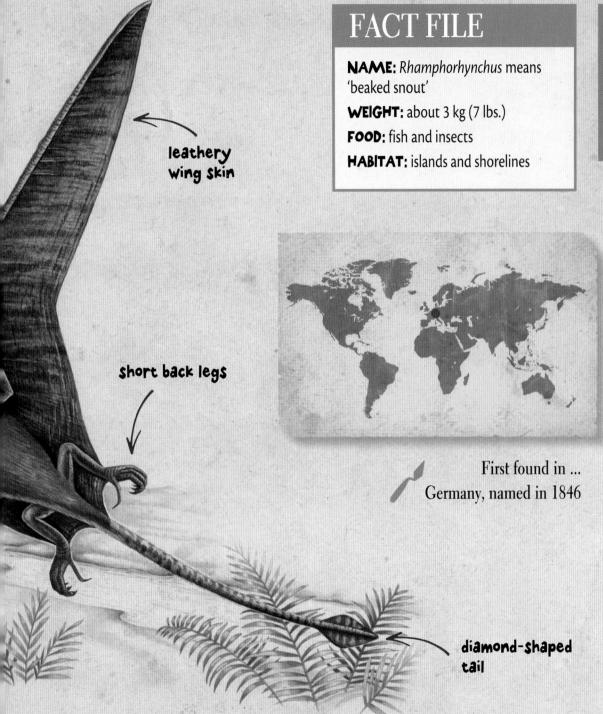

leathery
wing skin

FACT FILE

NAME: *Rhamphorhynchus* means 'beaked snout'
WEIGHT: about 3 kg (7 lbs.)
FOOD: fish and insects
HABITAT: islands and shorelines

short back legs

First found in ...
Germany, named in 1846

diamond-shaped
tail

21

Dinosaur quiz

Test your dinosaur detective skills!
Can you answer these questions?
Look in the book for clues.
The answers are on page 24.

2 What did this *pterosaur* eat?

1 Which *pterosaur* had two types of teeth?

3 Which reptile could glide from trees?

4 Which *pterosaur* probably walked on all fours?

Glossary

fossil
Part of an animal or plant in rock.
The animal or plant lived in ancient times.

habitat
The kind of place where an animal usually lives.

lagoon
A shallow pool near an ocean.

meat eater
An animal that eats
mostly meat.

pterosaur
A flying reptile with
wings and a long
wing finger.

wing finger
The fourth finger
on a pterosaur.
It held up a wing.

Find out more

Books

Dictionary of Dinosaurs: An Illustrated A to Z of Every Dinosaur Ever Discovered, Matthew G. Baron (Wide Eyed Editions, 2018)

The Big Book of Dinosaurs, DK Editors (DK Children, 2015)

Websites

www.bbc.co.uk/sn/prehistoric_life/dinosaurs

www.dkfindout.com/uk/dinosaurs-and-prehistoric-life

www.nhm.ac.uk/discover/watch-a-pterosaur-fly

Index

Quiz answers: 1. *Dimorphodon*. It had long front teeth and tiny back teeth.
2. *Anurognathus* ate insects. **3.** *Kuehneosuchus* could glide from trees.
4. *Pterodactylus*.